JUN   2008

W9-BYG-099

INDIAN MYTHOLOGY

FRED RAMEN

rosen publishing's
**rosen
central**

New York

To helen & Betty

Published in 2008 by The Rosen Publishing Group, Inc.
29 East 21st Street, New York, NY 10010

First Edition

Library of Congress Cataloging-in-Publication Data

Ramen, Fred.
Indian mythology/Fred Ramen.—1st ed.
    p. cm.—(Mythology around the world)
Includes bibliographical references and index.
ISBN-13: 978-1-4042-0735
ISBN-10: 1-4042-0735-X
1. Hinduism—Juvenile literature. 2. Mythology, India—Juvenile literature.
I. Title. II. Series.
BL1203.R68 2006
294.5'13—dc22

                                                                    2005030126

Manufactured in the United States of America

On the cover: A Hindu king *(left)* worships the blue-skinned god, Krishna, who was believed to bestow political authority on the nation's rulers.

CONTENTS

Introduction 4

1 The History of India 7

2 The World of Indian Mythology 17

3 Stories of the Gods and Goddesses 27

4 The *Ramayana,* or Journey of Rama 36

5 *The Mahabharata* 46

Glossary 56

For More Information 58

For Further Reading 60

Bibliography 61

Index 62

INTRODUCTION

The Indian subcontinent has been a center of civilization and culture since the dawn of recorded history. Presently home to nearly 1 billion people, India is emerging as a powerful player on the world's stage. It has the potential to be an economic giant with its own advanced technology.

But to many people in the Western world (Europe and the Americas), Indian culture remains a mystery. They rarely hear any of the more than 200 languages of India, and the religion and culture of the peoples of India seem alien and bewildering to them. But this does not have to be. There are more similarities between Indian and Western cultures than people are aware of. For instance, many of the languages of India, the Middle East, and Europe developed from a common language family called Indo-European. Also, the heroes and plots described in some stories and legends of India resemble those of European legends.

However, Indian mythology and legends have their own peculiar and fascinating character, and they richly reward the non-Indian reader who seeks them out. Myth and legend are very important to Indian culture. Hinduism, the religion of nearly a billion people worldwide (and the vast majority of the people of India), has preserved these stories in its sacred scriptures. Thus the epic tales of Rama or the Pandavas in the *Ramayana* and the *Mahabharata* are more than just great legends like the Greek *The Iliad* and *The Odyssey*;

An Indian woman shows off the mehendi decorations painted on her hands. The designs are made with henna dye. She is celebrating the Teej festival, which marks India's rainy season.

they are central to the beliefs of people from Mumbai to Bali, from Sri Lanka to New York City.

In Indian households to this day, children and parents gather to hear the stories of the heroes and gods. Often these are stories about the great hero Rama, who is held up as an example of the ideal man, warrior, and king. Other times, the stories may be from the *Mahabharata*, a vast treasure trove of myths, legends, and stories that is considered India's national epic. Or they may be funny and scary tales of Krishna, the blue god, who took on human form to kill demons and fight alongside the heroes of the *Mahabharata*. But the purpose of all these stories is greater than just entertainment: they are also examples of how to live (or not live) a good life. Today, through these myths, legends, and stories, young Hindus learn about deep spiritual truths. For the people of India, they form the basis of both cultural and religious education.

The stories and myths of India are a rich and varied tapestry unlike any other in the world. Step inside this world and be amazed, thrilled, and terrified, just as millions of others around the world have been for thousands of years.

1 THE HISTORY OF INDIA

Around 5,000 years ago, an advanced society arose in the Indus River valley. Today, this area makes up northwest India and Pakistan. We call the civilization that arose there the Indus Valley or Harappan civilization, after one of the major cities of the region.

Many of the religious traditions that would later be central to Hinduism come from the Indus Valley civilization. For example, Hindus place a high value on cleanliness and bathing, and at the center of many Indus towns there were large community baths. The bull was an important animal to the Indus Valley culture, just as cattle are sacred to present-day Hindus. A horned god appears in much religious artwork from this time, and modern scholars believe he is related to the Hindu god Shiva.

The people of the Indus Valley civilization may have been literate.

Indians view cows as sacred, as evidenced by this seventh-century sculpture of a cow wearing a wreath of flowers.

Some of the most common objects discovered in the ruins of their cities are ceremonial seals used to stamp objects, probably trade items. These seals are made of clay and usually have three or four symbols engraved on them. Whether or not these symbols were part of a true written language is still debated, however.

Although little is known about the religious practices of the Indus Valley people, some scholars think the Indus peoples worshipped a mother goddess associated with the earth. Archaeologists have found rough terra-cotta figurines that depict a woman, often pregnant, in nearly every home in the Indus Valley cities they have studied. Their society was apparently very stable and orderly, and there is little evidence of war or fighting.

The Collapse of the Indus Valley Civilization

Around 1900 BC, the Indus Valley civilization went into rapid decline. Within a century, most of the cities had been abandoned. It is not known exactly why this happened. Most researchers today believe there were multiple causes for the collapse. It seems that the climate became drier, making it harder to farm in the region. Also, a river that was important to agriculture may have dried up completely.

Soon after the decline of the Indus Valley civilization, a new people, the Aryans, arrived in the region. In Sanskrit, the word "Aryan" means "noble" or "honorable." In the 1930s, German Nazis used the word to refer to a Nordic, Caucasian "master race."

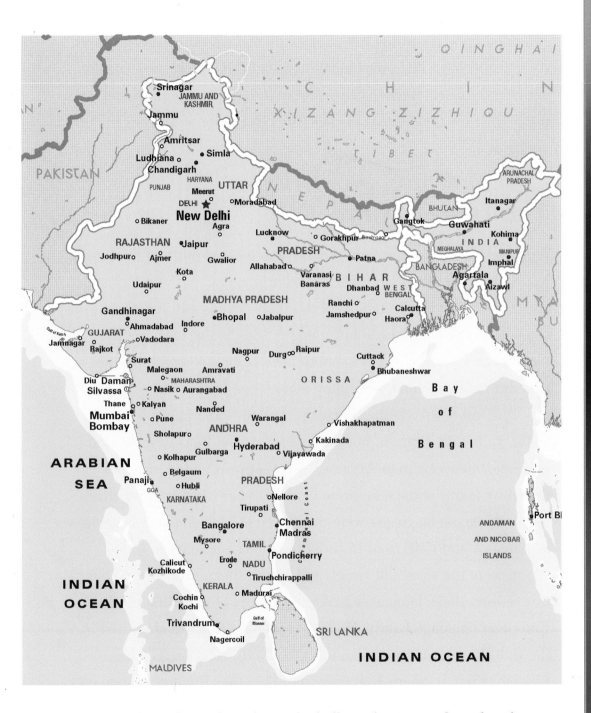

A map of the Indian subcontinent, including other parts of South Asia such as Sri Lanka, Pakistan, Nepal, Bangladesh, and part of China.

After that time, the word "Aryan" took on many negative connotations. As a result, most historians today now call the people who came to northern India the Indo-Aryans. They settled throughout the region, forming a new society that became the forerunner of modern Indian civilization.

The Indo-Aryans

The original land of the Indo-Aryans was located north of the Hindu Kush, the high mountain ranges in what is today northern Pakistan and Afghanistan. Descendants of the Indo-Aryans still live there and in present-day Iran, whose full name is Iran Shahr, meaning the "land of the Aryans." They seem to have been a nomadic people who did not farm much until they moved into India.

It is unknown whether horses played an important role in the Indus Valley civilization, but it is clear that the Indo-Aryans used horses extensively. Indo-Aryan chariots—two-wheeled war cars drawn by teams of horses—were central to how they fought battles.

Indo-Aryan languages were the source of such classical languages as Sanskrit and Pali, used in India. Languages related to Indo-Aryan were the source of Greek and Latin, spoken in Europe. For this reason, these languages make up what is often called the Indo-European language family. Modern languages that are classified in the Indo-European group also include Hindi, German, Gaelic, English, French, Spanish, Italian, and the other Romance languages based on Latin.

Indo-Aryan Religion and Vedic Culture

Unlike the Indus people, who probably worshipped an earth goddess, the Indo-Aryans believed in father gods associated with the sky. These sky gods of the Indo-Aryans became important figures in Hindu worship, while the female goddesses of the Indus people also took on major roles. Fire was an important element of Indo-Aryan worship. One of their most important gods was Agni, the god of fire. Burning offerings of food remains a part of Hindu ritual to this day.

After the Indo-Aryans moved into the region of northern India in greater numbers, a new culture emerged containing elements of both Indus and Indo-Aryan beliefs. This culture is known as Vedic culture, named after the major religious writings of the time, the Vedas.

The Vedas contain the basic myths of the creation of the world and the exploits of the gods. They also describe the rites and religious practices of Vedic worshippers, especially the priestly class, the Brahmins. The Vedas are composed in Sanskrit, the sacred language of the Indian people. The Vedas were solely the property of the Brahmins, and regular people were forbidden from learning these texts. For a long time, in fact, the Vedas were not written down and could be learned only by listening to someone who had memorized them. By about 1,500 years ago, however, they had been committed to writing.

Agni, the god of fire, is depicted in this seventeenth-century panel from a chariot used to carry Hindu idols on festival days.

Although many modern Hindu rituals and beliefs were passed down unchanged from the Vedic period, the Vedic religion was different from modern Hinduism. The gods Vishnu, Brahma, and Shiva were all relatively minor gods during this period. The celestial god Varuna and the sky god Indra were far more important. Then, between about 800 and 200 BC, the Upanishads were composed. These major religious works further redefined the religious beliefs of the people of India.

The Upanishadic Era

The Upanishadic period reflected the popular discontent with the central role of the priests and their complex rituals. Instead, the Upanishads taught a form of worship that could be accomplished by anyone willing to follow its principles.

Also during the Upanishadic period, many Indians came to believe that the various gods they worshipped were more like individual aspects of a universal god, Brahman. Brahman was identified with the world-soul, or atman, that was a part of every living thing in creation.

Another key belief that gained widespread acceptance during this time was the idea of samsara, or rebirth. For those who believe in samsara, nothing really dies; after death, the soul is reborn in a new form. This new form is determined by whether the person led a virtuous life. If the person led a bad life, he or she will suffer greatly in the new existence or even be born as an animal instead of a human being. On the other hand, an animal that lived a good

The Caste System

Among the changes in Indian society after the arrival of the Indo-Aryans was the introduction of the caste system. Castes are classes, or social divisions. There were four castes, or *varnas*, and many subcastes, or *jatis*. Each caste had certain duties to perform to keep society functioning, and only members of that caste were allowed to perform them. In order of importance, the castes were:

Brahmins: Brahmins were the priests, judges, and leaders of their communities. Only they could perform sacrifices and religious rituals. They wore white to symbolize their purity.

Kshatriyas: Kshatriyas were the warrior caste. They were also kings and rulers of countries. Kshatriyas traditionally wore red, for the blood they shed.

Vaishyas: The Vaishyas were farmers and merchants. They traditionally wore yellow, for the spices they grew and sold.

Shudras: The Shudras were the servant class. They traditionally wore blue or black to symbolize impurity.

Below the four recognized castes were the untouchables, or Dalits. Untouchables had almost no legal rights. They were allowed to do only the lowest and most degrading work, like cleaning stables or working in sewers. By the twentieth-century, many Indians opposed the caste system

Not only did Mohandas Gandhi attempt to end discrimination against "untouchables" and do away with India's rigid caste system, he also led a successful, nonviolent movement of resistance against British colonial rule of his nation.

saying it was unjust. Mohandas Gandhi (1869–1948) embraced the untouchables, renaming them Harijans or "people of God." In 1948, when India became independent from British colonial rule, it became illegal to discriminate based on caste. More than fifty years later, however, India's society is still greatly influenced by the caste system, and people in the lower castes are regularly subjected to poor treatment by those of the upper castes.

life can be reborn as a human, and a virtuous human can be reborn as a god. However, there is no escape from the cycle of birth, death, and rebirth as long as the person is tied to the material world. Only by rejecting materialism, by living humbly and sacrificing material comforts, can a person attain *moksha*, or release from the cycle of samsara.

Although the god Brahman became very important during the Upanishadic era, he is still only one part of a complex system of thousands of different divine beings. In the next chapter, we will meet some of these different gods and begin to learn about their roles in the huge body of Indian mythology.

2 THE WORLD OF INDIAN MYTHOLOGY

The world of Indian mythology shows the many influences of the cultures that preceded Indian civilization. These cultures include those of the Indus people, the Indo-Aryans, and the Mesopotamians. At the heart of Indian mythology, however, remains the creator god Brahman, the soul of the world.

Brahman

In classical Indian mythology, the world is a dream of Brahman, created and destroyed by him during every one of his days. At the end of one hundred years of Brahman, he too will be destroyed, and the universe will be

This is an ornate eleventh- or twelfth-century sculpture of the Indian god Vishnu.

in chaos until a new Brahman emerges to recreate it. Brahman has no reason to repeatedly create and destroy the universe, just as the universe has no reason for existing. The universe just is, and it has always existed.

Brahman is often interpreted through his different aspects: the three great gods Brahma (the creator), Vishnu (the sustainer), and Shiva (the destroyer). During each cycle, or *kalpa* (which lasts for one of Brahman's days), Brahman first creates the universe as Brahma, sustains it as Vishnu, and then destroys it as Shiva. Different sects of Hinduism revere only one of these individual aspects as the true aspect of Brahman. These sects, mostly devoted to Vishnu and Shiva, exist throughout India, although many Hindus today do not belong to any sect.

Hindu Goddesses: The Wives of the Gods

Each of the gods Brahma, Vishnu, and Shiva has a feminine counterpart, or wife. These counterparts are known as shaktis and are also considered aspects of Brahman. They are Shri or Lakshmi, wife of Vishnu and goddess of fortune and wealth; Parvati or Devi, wife of Shiva; and Saraswati, daughter and wife of Brahma. In Indian belief systems, the identities of the goddesses are much less separate than those of the gods. Parvati, in particular, is associated with divine female energy as embodied in the supreme goddess, Mahadevi Shakti.

The goddess Lakshmi appears in this painting on paper. Lakshmi, wife of the god Vishnu, is sitting on a lotus throne.

The Avatars of Vishnu

All of the gods of Indian belief have the ability to take on different forms, whether animal, human, vegetable, or force of nature. But only Vishnu actually descended into the world to be born, live, suffer, and die there. These incarnations are called avatars, from the Sanskrit word *avatara*, meaning "descent." Traditionally, there are ten avatars of Vishnu. Nine have already come, and the tenth will signal the end of the world.

One of the most important avatars of Vishnu is Krishna. In the Bhagavad Gita, a Hindu holy text, Vishnu, in the form of Krishna, says: "To protect the good, destroy the wicked, establish Dharma or right conduct on earth, I shall be born from age to age."

The avatars of Vishnu include the following:

1. Matsya, the fish who rescued the sage Manu from the flood that covered the world.
2. Kurma, the tortoise who dove to the bottom of the ocean to bring the gods back the elixir of immortality.
3. Varaha, the boar who pulled the earth back up from the bottom of the ocean, where a demon had thrown it.
4. Narasimha, a half-man, half-lion who killed a demon who could not be destroyed by man or beast.
5. Vamana, the dwarf who crossed the universe in three strides and saved all of creation from the demon Bali.
6. Parashurama, a human who prevented the Kshatriyas from becoming more powerful than the Brahmins.

7. Rama, the warrior king and hero of the *Ramayana*.
8. Krishna, the charioteer who slew the demon Kansa and fought for the Pandavas in the *Mahabharata*.
9. The Buddha, Siddhartha Gautama.
10. Kalki, a warrior who will come at the end of the world riding a white horse and holding a flaming sword.

In this painting, Vishnu, the sustainer god, appears as a four-armed man with a boar's head. This third avatar, or incarnation, of Vishnu is called Varaha. As he battles a sea demon, he holds symbols associated with Vishnu, including a conch shell, a club, a lotus, and a discus.

Three Major Gods

Brahma

Brahma is the creator of the universe, but he is not as important to later mythology as Vishnu and Shiva. There are various stories about why this is so. According to one, Brahma became obsessed with Saraswati, his daughter whom he created out of the energy of his mind. She tried to hide from him, but wherever she went, Brahma grew a new head in that direction, eventually ending up with five heads. Shiva then cut off the top head to show his displeasure with Brahma and further chided him because it was not fitting that he pursue his own daughter in this way. Because of this, Brahma is not worshipped on earth as Shiva and Vishnu are.

Vishnu

Vishnu preserves and sustains the universe. He often intervenes to aid humans and the other gods in fighting the demons and other forces of evil. Sometimes he does this by being born into the universe as a human or animal. These incarnations, or avatars, are very important in Indian mythology. Two of them—Rama and Krishna—are central characters in the great epics of Indian literature, the *Ramayana* and the *Mahabharata*.

Shiva

Shiva is revered as a god of opposites, and many Hindus believe him to be the true aspect of Brahman. Shiva has many different sides to him. He is usually depicted as a monk who has given up earthly, material desires. But he is also a god of fertility and the lord of wild dancing. He has a wife and children he is devoted to, providing Hindus with the ideal example of proper family life, yet he is also the destroyer who can wipe out the universe with a glance. He combines elements of the masculine and the feminine. For example, in his guise as Nataraja, the lord of the dance, he wears one male earring and one female earring.

The Devas

The other gods of Indian mythology are not thought of as aspects of Brahman. They are called *devas* ("shining ones")

Surrounded by a circle of flame, the destroyer god Shiva dances on the back of a dwarf named Apasmara. Apasmara represents ignorance, and Shiva crushes him to death during his dance.

and include many gods that were more important during the Vedic period. Varuna is a celestial god who guarantees the order of the universe. Indra, the king of heaven and ruler of the devas, is a sky god and warrior who strikes down his enemies with his thunderbolt. Yama, the god of the dead, rules hell, where the souls of the wicked must wait for their sins to be burned away so they can be reborn. Agni is the god of fire. Agni is a special deva because his smoke carries worshippers' sacrifices—usually food or incense—to the other gods.

Another important deva is Shiva's son Ganesha. Ganesha has the body of a chubby man and the head of an elephant. He is the god of success and new undertakings and is especially important to merchants.

There are many different stories about how Ganesha got his elephant's head. According to one, his mother, Parvati, asked the planet Saturn to babysit Ganesha. But the gaze of the goddess of Saturn was so powerful that when she looked at the baby, his head burst into flames. Shiva was sent out with orders to cut the head off of the first living thing that he met and use it to replace Ganesha's head. He came back with an elephant's head, which pleased Parvati, and since then Ganesha has had his present form.

The world that these gods inhabit is divided into three regions, usually called the Three Worlds (*triloka*). These are the physical world (*bhur*); the astral world, or the region of the stars (*bhuvar*); and heaven (*swarga*). The underworld, or hell, is part of the physical world. The universe is supported by eight elephants that stand on the back of a great turtle. This all important, universe-bearing turtle is an incarnation of Vishnu.

This eighteenth-century manuscript illustration depicts Indian women praying to Ganesha, the elephant-headed god of success and new undertakings.

Other Deities and Supernatural Beings

The three major gods—Brahma, Vishnu, and Shiva—and the devas are not the only supernatural beings in the world. Other gods, known as the *asuras*, are evil beings who oppose the devas and are constantly at war with them. The asuras are assisted by demons known as the *rakshasas*, who prey on human beings.

Humans, too, can attain supernatural power by fasting, praying, and meditating. Those who had done so to the point where they perceived the ultimate reality (the oneness of all things in Brahman) were called *rishis* or sages. The rishis were the authors of the Upanishads, which were composed over several centuries, and they had many powers. They could move freely among the Three Worlds, often appearing in a place as soon as someone summoned them with a thought. They could make the gods themselves appear before them and make them do their bidding. Rishis could also summon magical weapons of great power.

While the asuras were the enemies of the gods, they followed the same rituals as the devas; even evil demons chanted the Vedas and derived their power from them. The rishis could use the power they attained for both good and evil, and many of the gods feared the rishis because the rishis had become even more powerful than the gods themselves.

3 STORIES OF THE GODS AND GODDESSES

Most of the Indian myths you will read about in this book are derived from Hindu scripture. Specifically, they come from the Puranas (a collection of hymns and stories), the Vedas, and the vast collection of stories, poems, myths, and legends that make up the world's longest epic, the *Mahabharata*. These stories continue to be told to this day as part of Hindu rituals.

The following story from the Puranas is one of the most famous Indian myths. It contains some of the most important themes of Indian mythology: Vishnu as the preserver of the universe, Shiva's blue throat, the war between the devas and the asuras, and the idea that the devas' power is fragile and that they require outside assistance.

A section of the Sri Bhagavata Purana, a Vedic text, is recorded on this nineteenth-century scroll. It is written in Sanskrit and includes illustrations of Hindu myths.

The Churning of the Ocean

Long ago, when the world was still new, the god Indra, the ruler of heaven, insulted a great sage, Durvasa. In turn, Durvasa cursed Indra to weaken him. So holy was the great man that his curse immediately weakened all the gods, and their control over the world faded. Then the gods' enemies, the asuras, battled with them for control of the universe.

Finally, Indra and the other gods went to Vishnu, the great sustaining force of the universe. Vishnu realized that he had to act to restore balance to the universe.

"Take these herbs to the Milky Sea," said Vishnu, "and then take the sacred mountain Mandara and use it to churn the ocean. If you do these things, you will create nectar, the water of life, which will restore your power. You will need the help of the asuras. Promise them a taste of the nectar—I will make sure they get none."

So the gods made an alliance with their enemies. They took the great mountain Mandara and wrapped Vasuki, king of the serpents, around it. Then, with the demons on one side and the gods on the other, they churned the Milky Sea.

Many magical things came out of the ocean, including a poison deadly enough to destroy the world. Shiva snatched it up and drank it, which is why his throat is blue to this day. Finally, Dhanwantari rose from the sea, holding in his hands a cup of the water of life and the goddess Lakshmi, beloved of Vishnu. Vishnu later made Lakshmi his wife.

Under the direction of Vishnu, gods and demons churn the Milky Sea by wrapping Vasuki, king of the serpents, around the world's axis in this nineteenth-century painting.

The demons were furious that Lakshmi was favoring the gods, so they stole the nectar. But Vishnu took on the form of a beautiful woman and distracted the asuras long enough for him to steal back the water of life. When they drank it, the gods felt their power restored, and they freed the three worlds from the rule of the demons.

This first story in this chapter is about Vishnu. The next story is about Vishnu in the form of the blue god Krishna.

The Story of Krishna

Krishna's Birth and Escape

Once, long ago, there was a wicked king named Kansa. He had stolen the throne of his kingdom from his father, whom he locked in a dark prison. Kansa had a sister, Devaki, and he arranged a marriage for her with a man named Vasudeva. But just before the wedding, Kansa heard a terrible prophecy: the child of Devaki and Vasudeva would kill him.

Kansa was furious. But rather than kill his sister, he decided to kill all her children. He locked Vasudeva and Devaki in a cell together, and whenever they had a child, he would pick up the baby and throw it on the ground. Each time he did this, the infant would vanish in a flash of lightening.

The eighth child was named Krishna, which means "dark one." When Krishna was born, Vasudeva heard a voice telling him to carry the child to Gokul, across the Yamuna River. He found the door to his cell unlocked and his guards asleep, so he was able to escape from prison. As he waded across the river, it began to rise up—the river god recognized that Krishna was the avatar of Vishnu and wanted to touch him. Krishna stuck down his little foot and the river immediately parted, allowing his father to walk across to the other side.

Krishna, a Special Child

Vasudeva left Krishna with Yashoda, the wife of a cowherd. She raised the child as her own son. She knew nothing about his divinity or parentage. The young Krishna was very mischievous. He used to dance with the *gopis*, or milkmaids, and he used to steal butter from them and eat it. But he also showed that he was a special little boy. For example, the young Krishna told the people of his village that they should worship a mountain, not Indra, in order to receive good weather. This infuriated the king of heaven, so he sent rains for a full year to the village. But Krishna foiled Indra's plans, picking up the mountain and holding it over the town for the whole year to shield it from the rain.

When he was eleven, Krishna and his brother Balarama returned to Mathura, Kansa's kingdom. The evil king had laid a trap for the young boys, challenging them to a wrestling competition with his two huge champions, Chanur and Mustik. When the boys arrived, however, a great elephant charged them. (Kansa had no intention of letting them live.) Krishna leapt up on the elephant's back and strangled it. Then Chanur and Mustik attacked the boys, but Krishna killed Chanur, and Balarama killed Mustik. Krishna then grabbed Kansa and threw him against a wall, killing him. Krishna later became the new king.

Krishna later married 16,000 gopis and several other women— the number of marriages perhaps reflecting the incredible bounty and good fortune that Krishna brings. He became the king of

Dwarka, a magical kingdom that floated on the ocean. Later, he was also a very important figure in the events described in the *Mahabharata*.

Shiva's Eyes

Shiva's Third Eye

Like Vishnu, Shiva and his wife Parvati—also called Devi—have their own sects of worshippers who consider them to be the supreme deity. Shiva is often depicted with a third eye in the center of his forehead. He got this eye thanks to his wife, in her form of the beautiful goddess Uma, daughter of the Himalaya Mountains. One day while Shiva was deep in meditation, Uma playfully came up behind him and placed her hands over his eyes. Immediately, the universe was plunged into darkness. Then, suddenly, there was a light. A third eye opened in the middle of Shiva's forehead, and fire burst out of it, burning the Himalaya Mountains and destroying all the living things there. Uma

Krishna, the eight avatar of Vishnu, is viewed in Indian mythology as the supreme person and the highest god. He appears in this eighteenth-century illustrated manuscript surrounded by women and strolling in a garden.

removed her hands in shock, and Shiva closed his third eye and restored everything as it was, for he was all-forgiving.

This popular myth shows Shiva in all his aspects. He is the divine ascetic (hermit), meditating alone without any thought of worldly pleasures. He is also the devoted husband with a beautiful wife. At the same time, he is the terrifying destroyer of the universe as well as the gentle and good restorer of that universe. Shiva's third eye is a spiritual eye, able to see through the illusion of the world

Shiva *(right)* **sits beside his lover Umasahitamurti in this twelfth- to fourteenth-century bronze sculpture from southern India.**

into the true reality. As an aspect of Brahman, Shiva is that world, which is why the universe is plunged into darkness when Uma covers his eyes.

Devotion to Shiva

Shiva is said to be easy to please. Many of the other gods can only be worshipped by the higher castes, but anyone can worship Shiva and touch his images at the temple. He rewards devotion but has been known to test it severely. For example, there once was a low-caste hunter named Kannappa who was devoted to Shiva even though he did not know the proper rituals. Kannappa regularly brought offerings to an image of Shiva, so one day Shiva caused blood to flow from one of the eyes in his image. Kannappa tried everything to stop the bleeding but to no avail. Finally, he plucked out one of his own eyes and put it into the eye on the image, stopping the blood immediately. Soon after this, Shiva made the image's other eye bleed. Kannappa was about to gouge out his other eye when Shiva appeared to him, blessed him, and took him up to heaven.

These stories have concentrated on the activities of the gods. In the next two chapters, we will see how humans moved through the Three Worlds in two of the greatest epics in world literature—the *Ramayana* and the *Mahabharata*.

4 THE *RAMAYANA*, OR JOURNEY OF RAMA

The *Ramayana* is a great epic of India. The form of the story we know today emerged between 2,200 and 2,400 years ago. However, based on the astronomical references in the epic, some historians believe that the events in the story may have taken place as many as 5,000 years ago. The *Ramayana* consists of 24,000 lines of poetry in seven books, or *kandas*, and is still read and recited today. Throughout the great work, Rama represents the ideal hero, husband, and king. He is still held up as an example of how to live a good life as well as how to follow the rules of dharma, the divine law of the universe.

Ravana, the ten-headed king of Lanka, is the principal antagonist of the epic *Ramayana*.

Long ago, says the sage Valmiki at the start of the *Ramayana,* in the north of India there was a great kingdom called Koshala. The capital city of the kingdom was Ayodhya, and it was the greatest city in the world. Its king, Dasaratha, was the wisest ruler and strongest warrior in the world. He had been king for a long time and had made his people very happy, but one thing troubled him: he had no son to be his heir. He began a great ritual called the horse sacrifice in the hope that the gods would hear his prayer for a son.

At that very moment, the gods themselves were troubled and were meeting in Indra's heaven. A terrible demon named Ravana was oppressing the earth. From his great city of Lanka, Ravana and his demon army had spread out across the world, killing and eating innocent people. Yet the gods could do nothing to stop him because, in a moment of weakness, Brahma had made Ravana immune from the attack of both gods and demons.

Vishnu, hearing of the confusion and anguish of the gods, appeared before them, saying that he knew how to destroy Ravana: "What the gods cannot do, a human may certainly do."

"But," they said, "what human can hope to defeat such a powerful demon as Ravana? He has ten heads and twenty arms and knows many powerful spells."

"I myself will become that human," said Vishnu. In a flash he vanished and appeared to Dasaratha in the midst of a great bonfire. "Take this, O king," he said, offering some rice pudding. "Give it to your wives, and your wish will be fulfilled."

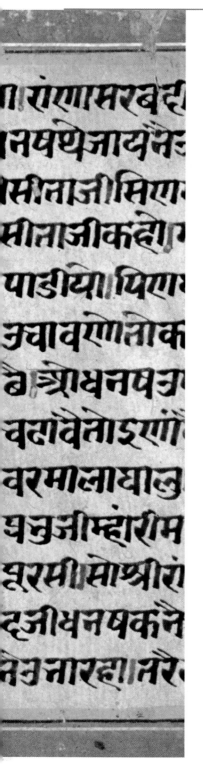

The Birth of Rama

Dasaratha had three wives. To his favorite, Kaushalya, he gave half the pudding, and she gave birth to a son named Rama. A third of the pudding went to Kaikeyi, Dasaratha's youngest wife, who gave birth to a son named Bharata. The rest of the pudding went to Sumitra, who bore twins, Lakshmana and Satrughana. These sons all shared some of Vishnu's divine power, but only Rama was Vishnu's true avatar.

Of all the sons, Rama and Lakshmana were the closest and were practically inseparable. When they were sixteen, a great sage came and took them into the forest, where he taught them how to kill demons and use magical weapons made by the gods. On their way home, they stopped in the city ruled by King Janaka. The king's daughter, Sita, was about to choose a husband from the suitors gathered around the palace. The man she chose had to be able to string a bow that belonged to Shiva. As it happened, no man was able to lift the bow,

Rama, surrounded by kings and holy men, prepares to string the bow in order to win Sita's hand in marriage in this manuscript illustration of a scene from the *Ramayana*.

Dharma and Karma

Dharma and karma are two central concepts of Hinduism. Dharma is moral law or duty. One way of understanding dharma is to see it as a code of proper behavior. But dharma is more than just a set of rules to be a good person; it is the fundamental law that binds the universe together. To go against dharma is to defy the universe. To follow it is to be in harmony with all things.

Karma, on the other hand, is the sum of all a person's acts. In Indian belief, karma extends into a person's past lives. The good fortune a person has in the present life results from good acts in a previous lifetime. Likewise, the suffering in this life is caused by misdeeds in an earlier existence. The way to get good karma is to follow dharma.

The ultimate goal of following dharma is to free one's self from samsara, the continuous cycle of birth, death, and rebirth. By erasing the debts of karma, a person can achieve moksha, or salvation, freedom from samsara.

This sculpture depicts one of the incidents of temptation experienced by Buddha, also known as Siddhartha Gautama, the ninth avatar of Vishnu. Buddha was tempted by Maara, a personification of evil and death, akin to Christianity's Satan.

let alone string it. But then Rama had his turn. He easily picked it up, bending it so far that it snapped in half. Sita then married the handsome prince, and they were very much in love.

Rama's Exile

Rather than wait until his own death, King Dasaratha decided to step down and hand over the kingdom to Rama, whom the people loved. But a maid overheard these plans and told Queen Kaikeyi. This made the queen afraid that her own son, Bharata, would be left without a place in the kingdom. In tears, Kaikeyi ran to Dasaratha, who promised to give her anything if she would stop crying.

"Then you must crown Bharata king, and exile Rama," she said.

Dasaratha was crushed; he could not go back on his word—but how could he banish his beloved son? Dasaratha lay in anguish all night, but in the end, he banished Rama to the forest for fourteen years. Rama, who always did anything his father asked, decided to leave immediately. He planned to leave alone, but Sita would not be separated from him. Lakshmana, too, begged to accompany his brother.

King Dasaratha was so distressed by what had happened that he died the night Rama went into the forest. When Bharata, who had been hunting in the mountains, returned to find out what had happened, he cursed his mother and refused to be king. He then put one of Rama's sandals on the throne and retired to a little hut to await his brother's return.

Ravana Steals Sita

Sita, Rama, and Lakshmana lived together in the forest and were happy. Before long, though, the demon Ravana heard of Sita's beauty and hatched a plan. He had one of his demons take on the form of a golden deer and appear to the three. When Rama and Lakshmana went off to chase it, Ravana himself came to Sita's hut in the form of a hermit. Before she realized who he was, Ravana snatched her up and flew through the air back to his city of Lanka.

Rama and Lakshmana took off in pursuit, but they had no trail to follow. In the mountains they met a great monkey named Sugriva. He offered to help Rama search for Sita if Rama would help Sugriva regain his monkey kingdom. Rama agreed, and together they returned Sugriva to the throne.

The Search for Sita

Since Rama had helped Sugriva, an alliance of monkeys and bears gathered and searched everywhere for Sita. One particularly clever monkey was Hanuman, the son of the wind god. He learned that Lanka was located far away, across the ocean (on the island we call Sri Lanka today). Summoning all his strength, he leapt across the ocean and landed in Lanka. Hanuman found Sita in a grove, surrounded by many fierce rakshasas. He told her Rama was coming, and she gave him a pearl to bring back so that Rama could be sure that it was his wife that Hanuman had met.

An eighteenth-century painting displays the joining of Rama and Sita following his successful completion of the bow-stringing challenge. Many myths and folktales involve a set of tasks and challenges that must be performed before a marriage can be allowed to go forward.

Hanuman then tore down the grove. Demons came, and he let himself be captured in order to meet Ravana and tell him to surrender. Ravana punished the monkey by setting his tail on fire. But Agni, the fire god, kept Hanuman from being hurt by the flames. Hanuman jumped from rooftop to rooftop until all of Lanka was on fire. Then he leapt back over the ocean to tell Rama where to find Sita.

Rama battles the ten-headed king of Lanka, Ravana, in this nineteenth-century painting on paper. Ravana had abducted Rama's wife, Sita. In retaliation, Rama killed all of Ravana's sons and soldiers, and eventually Ravana himself with an arrow through the heart.

The War with Ravana

The army of bears and monkeys followed Hanuman and Rama to the seashore. With the help of the ocean god, they built a bridge to Lanka.

For days, Rama and his monkeys and bears fought against the demons. Rama killed all of Ravana's sons and most of his brothers. However, many in Rama's army died as well. So Hanuman flew off to the Himalaya Mountains to find a magical herb that could bring them back to life. Unable to find the plant in the darkness, he pulled off the whole top of the mountain where the plant grew. Then he flew back to heal all the fallen monkeys and bears.

Finally, Ravana himself came out. He and Rama fought, each one sending showers of arrows at the other until, finally, Rama shot the demon in the heart.

Although Rama knew Sita has been faithful to him, he rejected her because he could not have her as his queen if people thought she had given in to Ravana's desires. To prove that she had been true, Sita jumped into a bonfire. When she emerged unhurt, Rama embraced her and the two returned to Ayodhya in triumph. Rama reigned for 11,000 years. He later waded into the holy river Ganges and returned to heaven as Vishnu, the Lord of the World.

5 THE *MAHABHARATA*

The *Mahabharata*, which can be translated as "great story of India," is the national epic. It is attributed to the sage Vyasa, who is also a major character in the poem. The *Mahabharata* is 100,000 stanzas long, or eight times longer than *The Iliad* and *The Odyssey* put together. It contains many different parts, including legends, stories, and myths, some of which you have already read about. It also contains instructions for how to worship the gods and a guidebook for kings to rule their kingdoms well. But at the heart of the *Mahabharata* is the story of the feud between the Pandavas and the Kauravas, two branches of the same family. To do justice to the story one would need a book much longer than the one you have in your hands. The following is but a brief summary of the main plot of the story.

Vyasa sits on an antelope skin while speaking to Narada, messenger of the gods.

The Pandavas and the Kauravas

A king named Pandu was suffering under a terrible curse because he accidentally killed a great rishi and his wife. The curse stipulated that Pandu would die immediately if he ever had children. He was sad because he would have no heirs, and for Indians, having a son is one of the most important things in life. Fortunately, his elder wife, Kunthi, knew a magic spell that allowed her to get pregnant by the gods. She bore three sons: Yudhisthira, the just, whose father was Yama, the benevolent god of the dead; Arjuna, the great warrior, whose father was Indra, the ruler of heaven; and Bhima, the strongest man in the world, fathered by Vayu, the god of wind.

Meanwhile, Pandu's blind older brother, Dhritarashtra, had 100 magical sons. The firstborn of these, Duryodhana, was wicked. He hated his cousins, the five sons of Pandu, who were called the Pandavas (three sons bore by Kunthi, and twins by Pandu's other wife Madri). After Pandu died, Dhritarashtra raised the Pandavas as his own sons. But Duryodhana continually schemed to make his branch of the family—known as the sons of Kuru, called the Kauravas—superior to them in every way.

Duryodhana's Plot

The Kauravas and the Pandavas were trained to be great warriors by Drona, a master of magic weapons. One day, Drona told them that their training was over. To pay his fee, they had to attack a king

The five brothers known as the Pandavas walk with their wife, Princess Draupadi, to Meru, the home of the Hindu gods.

named Drupada. King Drupada and Drona had grown up together. However, after becoming king, Drupada spurned Drona as inferior. Both the Kauravas and the Pandavas attacked Drupada, with the Pandavas succeeding when the Kauravas failed. Drona became king of half the kingdom, and Drupada swore revenge.

Humiliated by his enemy's victory in battle, Duryodhana decided to get rid of the Pandavas once and for all. He had his father send them to the city of Varanavata to rule over it. Then he plotted to kill them and their mother, Kunthi. Fortunately for them, their uncle Vidura warned them of the plot, and they escaped and went into hiding as beggarly Brahmins.

One day, they heard that princess Draupadi, daughter of King Drupada, was to choose her future husband. The Pandavas entered the contest, with Arjuna winning the hand of the beautiful girl. Around this time, Krishna, the king of Dwarka and avatar of Vishnu, became a fast friend of Arjuna.

The Gambling Match

Dhritarashtra heard that the Pandavas were in hiding, so he invited them back to his kingdom. He then gave them their own lands to rule, making sure this realm was an inhospitable desert. Despite this, the Pandavas' city, Indraprastha, became the envy of all the cities of the world. So Duryodhana again schemed to bring them down. Yudhisthira was a just and wise king, but he had one weakness: he loved to gamble, even though he was not good at it. Duryodhana challenged him to a game, and Duryodhana's uncle Sakuni, who had a pair of magic dice, won every game. Yudhisthira lost his entire kingdom and all his wealth. He and his brothers even lost their freedom.

Dhritarashtra eventually granted Draupadi's wish to restore all that the Pandavas had lost. Duryodhana was not finished, however. He again challenged Yudhisthira to a gambling match, and Yudhisthira could not refuse the request. When he lost again, he and his fellow Pandavas went into exile for thirteen years. Eventually, the Kauravas regretted what they had done, for they knew the Pandavas would take their revenge as soon as the exile ended.

The Kalpas

According to Hindu belief, the world is created and destroyed each day. Fortunately, the day is not one of our days, but a day of Brahman, the creator and soul of the universe. Each day of Brahman lasts an unbelievably long time: 4,320,000,000 years! At the end of the day, the world is destroyed and lies in chaos for a night that lasts as long as the day. At the end of the night, Brahman takes on the forms of Brahma, Vishnu, and Shiva and recreates the universe. This cycle is called the kalpa and is divided into other parts. There are fourteen manvantaras during each kalpa; at the end of the manvantara, the world is drowned in a flood. In each manvantara, a great teacher, the Manu, emerges to start the human race over again, teaching and enlightening people.

The kalpa is also divided into 1,000 yuga cycles. There are four parts to each yuga: the Satya yuga, when humans are at their most spiritual and which lasts 1,728,000 years; the Treta yuga, an age of mental accomplishment that lasts 1,296,000 years; the Dvapara yuga, an age of great inventions that lasts 864,000 years; and the present yuga, the Kali yuga, when people are focused on mere survival and cannot perceive the spiritual world easily. The Kali yuga lasts 432,000 years; ours began in 3100 BC.

Traditions say that the events of the *Ramayana* took place in the Treta yuga, while those of the *Mahabharata* took place in the Dvapara yuga. While modern Indian scientists and historians do not take these numbers literally (the events of the *Ramayana* are thought to have taken place perhaps as many as 5,000 years ago), the kalpa and yuga cycles remain important parts of Indian astrology and Hindu belief.

The *Mahabharata* War

So it was. After hiding for the appointed time, the Pandavas regrouped and summoned up a great army. They marched on the Kauravas, who gathered their own army, and the two sides met on the field of Kurukshetra. On the eve of the battle, Arjuna lost heart because so many men were about to die. But Krishna, who was Arjuna's charioteer, delivered a great speech, revealing his nature as Vishnu and explaining how the universe works. (This explanation makes up the text of the classic Bhagavad Gita, one of the great works of Indian religious literature.)

The ensuing battle lasted eighteen days, and many men died on both sides. The Pandavas had many obstacles to overcome. First, their great-uncle Bhishma fought against them. Finally, the Pandavas were able to paralyze him when Arjuna filled him with so many arrows that he lay on them like a bed. (In a later section of the *Mahabharata*, Yudhisthira meets with the dying Bhishma and learns much about how to be a good king.) Bhishma was succeeded by Drona, their old weaponsmaster, who wanted to stay neutral but

ended up fighting for the Kauravas because his son, Aswathma, was a friend of Duryodhana.

None of the Pandavas could defeat Drona, either, so they resorted to trickery. Yudhisthira was known to be honest, so he shouted out that Aswathma, Drona's son, had been killed. Actually, it was an elephant of that name that had died, but Yudhisthira said the word "elephant" so softly that Drona could not hear it. Drona lost heart and was killed by Drupada's son, Dhrishtadyumna.

After the War

In the end, Duryodhana was one of only a few warriors left on the Kauravas' side. Yudhisthira, who could never resist gambling, offered him one last chance: fight against any one of the Pandavas, and the winner would get the kingdom. Bhima and Duryodhana fought, and Bhima won only by treacherously hitting Duryodhana in the thigh, a target that was normally considered off

Krishna and the reluctant Arjuna head into battle against the Kauravas, the sons of Dhritarashtra. Arjuna was a master archer and the third of the five Pandava brothers who were so hated by the Kauravas.

limits. Even in dying, Duryodhana was defiant, urging the few surviving members of the Kauravas to continue fighting the Pandavas.

Six million men died in the battle, and only a handful survived. Afterward, the Pandavas ruled the kingdom in peace. Krishna died years later in a forest, accidentally killed by a hunter while he sat meditating. After Krishna's death, his kingdom of Dwarka sank into the ocean. After thirty-six years, the Pandavas and Draupadi set off for heaven. All of them died on the way except for Yudhisthira, who arrived with a dog in his hands. The gatekeeper of heaven told him to leave the dog behind, but he refused. The dog then turned out to have been the god Dharma.

As a final test from the gods, who wanted to see if Yudhisthira was truly worthy of entering heaven, Yudhisthira was made to see only the Kauravas when he arrived in heaven. His brothers and Draupadi were in hell, he was told. Without hesitating, Yudhisthira asked to be sent to hell as well. At that point, he was reunited with his family in heaven, and there the *Mahabharata* ends.

In Conclusion

Indian mythology is unlike many other world mythologies because even now it continues to be seen as a living, breathing, still-developing entity and an everyday source of religious inspiration. Throughout the Hindu world, people still learn about Rama and Arjuna. Children still laugh at the merry antics of Hanuman and dream

Hindus celebrate the Holi festival, a festival of color. During the festivities, celebrants cover themselves in dyed water and brightly colored powder. The festival, associated with Krishna, celebrates the arrival of spring.

about Krishna's dances with the gopis. They also continue to tremble at the evil deeds of Ravana and Kansa.

While the *Mahabharata* and the *Ramayana* are still not widely read outside of India, they are nonetheless recognized as classics of world literature, deeply inspirational stories that offer valuable ethical lessons as well as thrilling stories of gods, goddesses, and human heroes and heroines. Entering into the world of Indian mythology is a richly rewarding experience, one that will provide readers with a rich, fascinating, mysterious, magical store of literary and cultural treasures.

GLOSSARY

atman The soul or breath of the universe, identified with Brahman.

avatar From the Sanskrit for "descent," an earthly incarnation of a Hindu god.

Brahma Hindu god; the creator aspect of Brahman.

Brahman The creator god, the soul of the universe who is one with all things.

Brahmins Members of the priestly caste in India.

caste One of the classes or divisions in Indian society.

dharma The basic principles of nature and divine law in Hinduism.

epic A long poem that celebrates heroic deeds.

Ganesha The elephant-headed god of prosperity; the son of Shiva and Parvati.

Hindi One of the major languages of modern India.

Hindu One who believes in the divine law of dharma; generally, a person from India.

Hindu Kush A region of high mountains between modern-day Pakistan and Afghanistan.

incarnation A human or animal form taken by a god.

Indo-Aryans People from the region of modern-day Iran who moved into northwestern India approximately 4,000 years ago.

karma The sum of all a person's acts in past, present, and future lives; the effects of these acts and the way they create or determine past, present, and future.

Krishna A key avatar of Vishnu.

Lakshmi Vishnu's wife; the goddess of prosperity and fortune.

Mahabharata The great national epic of India; a vast compendium of myth, legend, rituals, advice for rulers, and prayers. It also includes the story of the feud between the Pandavas and Kauravas.

Parvati Shiva's wife, also known as Devi or Uma; she is identified with the mother goddess of the Indus Valley civilization.

Ramayana The great epic story of Prince Rama, an incarnation of Vishnu, and his war against the rakshasa Ravana.

samsara The cycle of birth, death, and rebirth.

Sanskrit The sacred language of India. No longer spoken in everyday life, it is preserved as the language of the Vedas, the *Ramayana*, and the *Mahabharata*.

Shiva Hindu god; the destructive aspect of Brahman.

Shri The wife of Vishnu; also known as Lakshmi.

subcontinent A large subdivision of a continent, such as the one occupied by present-day India and Pakistan. The region is called a subcontinent because it is geographically distinct from the rest of Asia and separated from central Asia by high mountains.

Upanishads Sacred writings composed after the Vedas that offered a new way to reach salvation without relying on priestly ritual.

Vedas The sacred scriptures of the early Indo-Aryan civilization; still a part of modern Hinduism.

Vishnu Hindu god; the sustaining aspect of Brahman.

■ FOR MORE INFORMATION

American Hindu Association
P.O. Box 55405
Madison, WI 53705
Web site: http://www.americanhindu.net

Asia Society and Museum
725 Park Avenue
New York, NY 10021
(212) 288-6400
Web site: http://www.asiasociety.org

Indian Council for Cultural Relations
26/3B, Sankey Road
Bangalore 560 052
Karnataka
India
Web site: http://www.education.vsnl.com/iccr

Indo-American Society
5 D. Sukhadwala Marg
Fort Mumbai 400 001
India
E-mail: indam@vsnl.com
Web site: http://www.indoamericansociety.org

South Asia Center
University of Pennsylvania
820 Williams Hall
36th and Spruce Streets
Philadelphia, PA 19104-6305
(215) 898-7475
Web site: http://www.southasiacenter.upenn.edu/index.htm

Web Sites

Due to the changing nature of Internet links, Rosen Publishing has developed an online list of Web sites related to the subject of this book. This site is updated regularly. Please use this link to access the list:

http://www.rosenlinks.com/maw/indi

FOR FURTHER READING

Daniélou, Alain. *The Myths and Gods of India: The Classic Work on Hindu Polytheism* (Princeton Bollingen Series). Rochester, VT: Inner Traditions, 1991.

Devi, Vanamali. *The Play of God: Visions of the Life of Krishna.* San Diego, CA: Blue Dove Press, 1995.

Jaffrey, Madhur. *Seasons of Splendour: Tales, Myths and Legends of India.* New York, NY: Atheneum, 1985.

Novesky, Amy, and Belgin K. Wedman. *Elephant Prince: The Story of Ganesh.* San Rafael, CA: Mandala Publishing, 2004.

Pattanaik, Devdutt. *Indian Mythology: Tales from the Heart of the Subcontinent.* Rochester, VT: Inner Traditions, 2003.

Wangu, Madhu Bazaz. *Hinduism.* New York, NY: Facts on File, 1991.

BIBLIOGRAPHY

Beck, Brenda E. F., Peter J. Claus, Praphulladatta Goswami, and Jawararlal Handoo, eds. *Folktales of India.* Chicago, IL: University of Chicago Press, 1987.

Coomaraswamy, Ananda K., and Sister Nivedita. *Myths of the Hindus and Buddhists.* New York, NY: Dover Publications, 1967.

Naryan, R. K. *The Mahabharata: A Shortened Prose Version of the Indian Epic.* Chicago, IL: University of Chicago Press, 1978.

Prime, Ranchor. *Ramayana: A Journey.* London, England: Collins and Brown, 1997.

Storm, Rachel. *Mythology of India.* London, England: Anness Publishing, 2000.

⬛ INDEX

A

Afghanistan, 10
Agni, 24
ascetic, 34
asuras, 25, 27, 28, 29
atman, 13
avatar, 20, 22

B

Bhagavad Gita, 20, 51
Brahma, 13, 18, 22, 25, 37
Brahman, 13, 16, 17–18, 22, 23, 26,
        35, 50
Brahmins, 11, 14, 20, 47
Buddha, 21

D

Dalits, 14
dharma, 20, 36, 40, 54
Durvasa, 28

G

Ganesha, 24
Gautama, Siddhartha (the Buddha), 21
Ghandi, Mohandas, 15
gopis, 31, 54

H

Harappan civilization, 7
Harijans, 15
Himalaya Mountains, 33, 45

I

The Iliad, 4, 46
incarnation, 20, 22, 24

India
    caste system, 14–15, 35
    family life, 5, 23
    great epic of, 5, 36
    history of, 7–8, 10–11, 13–16
    languages, 4, 8, 10, 11
    population, 4
    similarities with Western culture,
        4–5, 10
Indian mythology
    devas, 23–24, 27
    goddesses, 11, 18, 55
    rituals, 8, 11, 13, 27, 35, 37
    role of, 4, 6,
    secondary beings, 25–26
    themes of, 27–31
three major gods of, 22–23, 25
Indo-Aryans, 10–11, 13, 17
Indo-European, 4
Indra, 13, 24, 28, 31, 47
Indus Valley, 7, 8

K

kalpas, 50, 51
kandas, 36
Kannappa, 35
Kansa, 21, 30, 31, 55
karma, 40
Krishna
    as an avatar of Vishnu, 20, 21, 22
    identity of, 30, 51
    story of, 30–31, 33
Kshatriyas, 14

L

Lakshmi, 28, 29

M

Mahabharata, 4, 5, 6, 21, 22, 27, 33, 35, 46–51, 53–55
meditation, 26, 34, 54
Mesopotamians, 17
moksha, 40

N

Nataraja, 23

O

The Odyssey, 4, 46

P

Pakistan, 7
Pali, 10
Parvati, 18, 24, 33
Puranas, 27

R

rakshasas, 25, 42
Rama, 4, 5, 22, 36, 39, 41–43, 45
Ramayana, 4, 21, 22, 35, 36–37, 39, 41–43, 45, 50, 51, 55
Ravana, 55
rishis, 26, 47

S

salvation, 40
samsara, 13, 16, 40
Sanskrit, 8, 10, 11, 20
shaktis, 18
Shiva
    in the hierarchy of worship, 22
    identity of, 7, 18, 22–23
    third eye of, 33–35
Shuras, 14
Sita, 39, 41, 42–43, 45
Sri Lanka, 5, 42
subcontinent, 4

U

Upanishads, 13, 16, 26

V

Vaishyas, 14
Vedas, 11, 13, 27
Vishnu
    avatars of, 20–21, 24, 39, 49
    in the hierarchy of worship, 22
    identity of, 18, 22, 27, 28, 45
    wives of, 28

About the Author

Fred Ramen studied English and comparative literature at Hofstra University. He is the author of *The Historical Atlas of Iran*, also by Rosen Publishing, Inc. He maintains a longstanding interest in Asian culture and is a practitioner of the martial art aikido. Ramen lives in New York City and was recently a participant in the *Jeopardy!* Ultimate Tournament of Champions.

Photo Credits

Cover © The British Museum/Topham-HIP/The Image Works; p. 5 © Kamal Kishore/Reuters/Corbis; pp. 7, 48 Erich Lessing/Art Resource, NY; p. 9 © ILLUSTRATOR MAP; pp. 12, 23, 43 Victoria and Albert Museum, London/Art Resource, NY; p. 15 © AFP/Getty Images; p. 17 The Art Archive/Musée Guimet Paris/Dagli Orti; p. 19 Ann and Bury Peerless Picture Library, Private Collection/The Bridgeman Art Library; p. 21 © The British Museum/Topham-HIP/The Image Works; pp. 25, 46, 52–53 Bildarchiv Preussischer Kulturbesitz/Art Resource, NY; pp. 27, 44 HIP/Art Resource, NY; p. 29 The Art Archive/Victoria and Albert Museum London/Eileen Tweedy; pp. 32–33 The Art Archive/Bodleian Library Oxford; p. 34 Réunion des Musées Nationaux/Art Resource, NY; p. 36 The Stapleton Collection, Private Collection/The Bridgeman Art Library; pp. 38–39 © Burstein Collection/Corbis; p. 40 Scala/Art Resource, NY; p. 55 © Lindsay Hebberd/Corbis.

Designer: Tom Forget; **Editor:** Wayne Anderson
Photo Researcher: Amy Feinberg